You Can Do Anything

Danni Maynard

You Can Do Anything
Copyright © 2021 by Danni Maynard

All rights reserved. No part of this publication may be reproduced, distributed, or transmitted in any form or by any means, including photocopying, recording, or other electronic or mechanical methods, without the prior written permission of the author, except in the case of brief quotations embodied in critical reviews and certain other non-commercial uses permitted by copyright law.

Tellwell Talent
www.tellwell.ca

ISBN
978-0-2288-4202-6 (Hardcover)
978-0-2288-4201-9 (Paperback)

This book is dedicated to four amazing kids:

Deklin, Lachlan, William and Evelyn.

Last night I had a dream of all the things I could be: a pilot, a lawyer, and a captain at sea.

In my dream was my brother, he was there too. He was a dancer, a nurse and a vet at the zoo.

My mum told me, when Great-Grandma was small, boys only did boys things and girls couldn't at all.

Girls would clean houses, cook dinner and go shopping. They couldn't fly planes, drive trucks or do doctoring.

When I am a lawyer I will stand up and be proud. I will shout to the world, "I can be anything," OUT LOUD.

To the airport I'll go and fly in the sky, because I am a pilot who loves being up high.

On weekends I will sail to the sea and the ocean, my smile will be huge when the waves are in motion.

It is great to be a girl in the world of today, I can be anything and I still get to play.

When I'm tucked up in my bed with my blanket so tight, I can't wait to see what I dream of tonight.

The End

www.ingramcontent.com/pod-product-compliance
Lightning Source LLC
LaVergne TN
LVHW071733060526
838200LV00031B/486